ENVIRONMENTAL
ISSUES

BookLife
PUBLISHING

By Emilie Dufresne

BookLife
PUBLISHING

©2019
BookLife Publishing Ltd.
King's Lynn
Norfolk, PE30 4LS

ISBN: 978-1-78637-600-8

Written by:
Emilie Dufresne

Edited by:
Kirsty Holmes

Designed by:
Amy Li

CONTENTS

Words that look like **this** can be found in the glossary on page 24.

WHAT IS A DISASTER?

A disaster is a sudden event that causes a lot of damage to the **environment** and human life. They are very dangerous events that cause many problems.

Big disasters can be very expensive to fix. This can make the effects of the disaster last longer. This is because people may not be able to afford the time, money and helpers needed to recover.

CHARITIES OFTEN COME AND GIVE FOOD, WATER AND MEDICAL AID TO VICTIMS.

TYPES OF DISASTER

There are two types of disaster: natural and environmental.

Natural disasters are disasters that happen because of natural causes. Some examples of natural disasters are earthquakes, floods and volcanic eruptions.

Environmental disasters are disasters that happen because of human actions. Some examples of environmental disasters are oil spills, chemical explosions and gas leaks.

LET'S LOOK AT SOME DIFFERENT TYPES OF ENVIRONMENTAL DISASTER.

INDUSTRIAL DISASTERS

The word 'industry' means the factories, machines and processes that are used to create different products.

ANY DISASTER THAT IS RELATED TO INDUSTRY IS KNOWN AS AN INDUSTRIAL DISASTER.

OIL SPILLS HAPPEN WHEN SHIPS LEAK THE OIL THEY ARE CARRYING.

Industrial disasters include nuclear explosions, gas leaks and oil spills. These disasters are often accidents, or happen because **equipment** isn't looked after properly.

Industrial disasters can cause a lot of damage to plants, animals and humans. Oil doesn't mix with water, so when an oil spill happens, the oil floats on top of the water.

THE OIL IS VERY HARD TO CLEAN UP AS IT STICKS TO WHATEVER IT TOUCHES, LIKE THIS BIRD.

IT CAN BE HARD FOR PLANTS AND ANIMALS TO SURVIVE IN AREAS WHERE INDUSTRIAL DISASTERS HAPPEN.

Oil spills, gas leaks and nuclear explosions release dangerous materials into the environment. This can **contaminate** the area with **hazardous** materials.

AGRICULTURAL DISASTERS

The word 'agriculture' means the machinery, fields, animals and plants that are used to help us produce food.

THERE ARE LOTS OF DIFFERENT TYPES OF AGRICULTURAL DISASTER.

Agricultural disasters can be caused by over or under watering an area, ploughing the land too much, or overusing **pesticides**.

THESE CAN ALL CAUSE SERIOUS PROBLEMS FOR THE ENVIRONMENT.

Some pesticides are dangerous to humans and animals. They can build up in the soil, making it harder for the crops to grow. Ploughing and over or under watering can also make the land **barren**.

It takes a long time for the soil to get back all the **nutrients** it loses from being watered, ploughed and sprayed with pesticides.

BIODIVERSITY DISASTERS

Biodiversity means having lots of different types of animals and plants in one area. Having good biodiversity is better for the **ecosystem**.

CANE TOADS WERE INTRODUCED TO AUSTRALIA TO CONTROL PESTS.

Biodiversity disasters often happen when humans introduce a new animal or plant to an area that they don't normally live in. This is often done to control a **native species**.

Introduced species often eat the food and take the homes of lots of native species. This might make it hard for the native species to survive there.

GREY SQUIRRELS WERE INTRODUCED TO THE UK IN THE 1870S. THEY TAKE A LOT OF FOOD AND SHELTER THAT THE NATIVE RED SQUIRRELS NEED.

This Ko'ko' bird is now **endangered** because the brown tree snake was introduced to its environment. Like many introduced species, the snake has no **predators** and is quickly growing in numbers.

AFTER AN ENVIRONMENTAL DISASTER

Environmental disasters have long lasting effects on the planet. For example, plant and animal life might never adjust to an introduced species after a biodiversity disaster.

RED SQUIRREL NUMBERS ARE STILL FALLING SINCE GREY SQUIRRELS WERE INTRODUCED.

SITE OF NUCLEAR EXPLOSION

CAUTION

RADIOACTIVE MATERIALS

After an industrial disaster, dangerous chemicals can be found in the area for years and years afterwards. These areas can become so dangerous that humans can no longer visit them.

ENVIRONMENTAL DISASTER FACTS

One way to get rid of oil on the sea is to burn it. This does get rid of the oil but it also releases harmful gases into the environment.

A nuclear disaster that happened in Ukraine in 1986 could be contaminated with radiation for around 300 years.

42% of all endangered species are at risk because of introduced animals and plants.

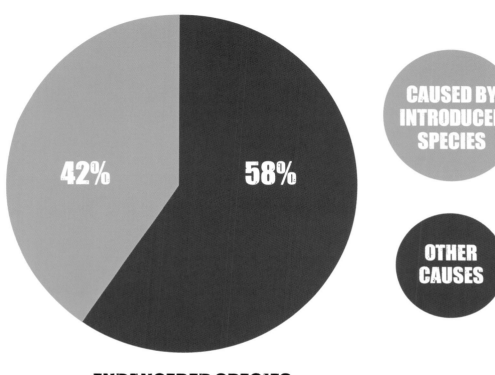

42%

58%

CAUSED BY
INTRODUCED
SPECIES

OTHER
CAUSES

ENDANGERED SPECIES

If there are dangerous chemicals in an area people might have to wear **hazmat suits**. These stop people from becoming ill from the chemicals.

GLOSSARY

barren	not able to produce, or support the growth of crops
contaminate	to make something unclean by adding a harmful substance to it
ecosystem	a community of living things and the environment they live in
endangered	when a species of animal is in danger of going extinct
environment	the natural world
equipment	items that are needed to complete a certain job
hazardous	something that has great risk or danger
hazmat suits	full-body suits that protect people
native species	an animal or plant that originally came from an environment or ecosystem
nutrients	natural substances that plants and animals need to grow and stay healthy
pesticides	chemicals used to kill animals and insects that damage crops
predators	animals that hunt other animals for food

INDEX

Photocredits – Images are courtesy of Shutterstock.com. With thanks to Getty Images, Thinkstock Photo and iStockphoto.
Cover – Buffy1982, Thanakrit Homsiri, 1 – IhorL, 2 – fboudrias, 3 – IrinaK, 4 – austinding, 5 – Chris Warham, 6 – Doug McLean, 7 – sandyman, 8 – leungchopan, 9 – Tigergallery, 10 – Mike Shooter, 11 – David Bailey, 12 – Fotokostic, 13 – vesilvio, 14 – Byelikova Oksana, 15 – Chukov, 16 – Anjo Kan, 17 – Patrick K. Campbell, 18 – Patrik Mezirka, 19 – Greg Hume (wikipedia), 20 – Giedriius, 21 – vasakkohaline, 22 – Forrest Dix, Kaspri, 23 – Martin Lisner.